THE INDICATIVE ACT, 2022

LIBERALIZATION OF INDIAN ECONOMY AND IT'S AFTER EFFECT

KUMAR ABHISHEK

I DEDICATE THIS BOOK TO ALL THE PROMINENT SOCIAL REFORMERS OF THE PAST 30 YEARS OF INDIA.

Contents

Preface

This book is about our real economic struggle and social reform of India.It revolves around the economic liberlization and the after effect that leads to develop our country India.It recognises our efforts to connect India and the world with a open frame of mind that could capture the imgination of the world and our country.This book also helps the foreign nations to understand Indian perspective about the world and clarify the vision.It involves the key creation of the social and democratic view and with our economic potential.One of the chapter also recognises how to resolve the menace, Terrorism.It also have a vision of India's foreign policy and how it drives around the world.

CHAPTER ONE

THE TRANSITION

POCKET DEFINITION 0F ECONOMIC LIBERALIZATION OF INDIA, 1991

"The economic liberalization in India refers to the economic liberalization of the country's economic policies initiated in 1991 with the goal of making the economy more

market and service oriented and expanding the role private and foreign investment".(Note:quote reference taken from wikipedia).

MY INTERPRETATION

Before I start dreaming about my completion of book one day.I want to convey my readers to inculcate about the book such that they are left with the synchronization

of deeds and myth as well as well as good reads.I have experienced many economics to substantially generate new ideas, thinking, giving and taking, facilitate doors

of new possibilities and last but not the least making consensus from people.I want to assure that among every story there is a satisfactory end in general.

my first topic to take part in discussion with competent and knowledgeable and at the same time try to convince the disagreement is actually "from where that kind of

situation comes into play so that it become a need for stabilizingp the economic liberalization in India".

See before I indulge in saying that "economics is the game of snakes and ladders involved".

I say so because economy is a fragile agreement which can take you to volatile when it needs to be level up by the ladders.And sometimes it may can be the reason for downfall and slip to lower level by the snakes .all in all here it is laid to be conveyed like a pulley balance while taking risk people world over say business as

usual after 1991 is a more risk taking venture or event.Indian economy is not far from it.It is the mirror of the statement that "economics is the subject of snakes

and ladders".

WHY ECONOMY?

Economy is actually the solution to the problem arises due to unstable and unequal distribution of wealth.It is a curriculum or index or ruling to envasagel equality in

terms of narrowing the gap between rich and poor.It is a business which allows prosperity of one and regularizes that wealth spent and rotate in business of give and

take and sometimes borrow also, which need trust business .This is how business is done in an economy like India.

Indian economy has embedded and evolved simultaneously to cope the snakes and use the ladder all the way...

Economy is in everything, it is like a support system of the life for making life a easier and simplified.In earlier days economy were based on giving and taking

commodities like taking rice in in return of other crops or vegetable or spices.It was the way of business and market to appoint things according to their views and

evaluation. Then come the culture of money which "simplified everything".

Firstly, it was of gold and silver according to its face value And later on it is the "make believe behind basic".

for the purposes govt.or rulers started the value of royalty and get paid as tax for ruling and providing security, justice, a market and equality.The process evolved

and the procedure simplified later on and now currency does the jobs agreement of give and take.

INDIA BEFORE LIBERALIZATION

ECONOMY IS NOT ABOUT LIVING ON THE EDGE BUT BALANCING AT THE CENTRE,STANDSTILL AND VOLATILE AND FLEXIBLE.Before liberalization, India and Indian govt gone through a first transition after independence.This transition includes the industrialization of steel, electricity, construction of dams,aluminium and copper industries coal

industry(mining), research centres, scientific revolutions, infrastructure industry, railways, airports, roads , village roads, NH roads, and the list is endless and got

nationalized before 1991.Also "private public partnership" for making waterways, insurance, and mining are located and gone through first transition, or nationalized

too.INDIA made noted establishment and progress but then also the challenges of world order economy were needed to escape...

Resembling centre planning of soviet union India also made and defined and regulated our economy and marked with a five year plan.

ACCORDING TO BBC...

Before the process of reform began in 1991, the govt.attempted to close the economy for outside elaborating licences regulation and red tap culture referred to

licence raj were required to set up business in India before liberalisation. Licence raj and imposes high tariff and import licence prevented foreign goods.

Limitation In Detail The most tragic shell in the history of liberalization is of Indian economic liberalization.It cannot defy the attraction of modern world before 1991.The economic libration brought a freedom unless of autarky.Growth alone is a deep gorge in the world of economy, falling in it when required to be breaking stereo types and moving with the world would be the fruits of our independence struggle.Our forefathers had chosen the complete swarajya but there was a compulsion that India and Indians should should also experienced the developed culture, heritage and social structure too with the Indianess and India's rich past. India is land of Ashoka, Chandragupta Mourya, Shiva ji, as well as Mahatma Gandhi, Jawahar lal Nehru, Sardar Vallabhbhai patel.This is the varistion of Indianess that both the structure are equally important, this diversity is actually derived from different kind of rulers includes Muslim rulers, Mughal Rulers, East India company and so on... All had a contribution and PART OF THE HISTORY OF INDIA, from where evolved as nd surfaced to a country like India, Now India is in the every world stage and residing in the bubbles of international command.Also every foreign country enjoy friendship with India and knocking the doors of business industrialization and social bonding in the light of india as a secular state respecting every other culture, bonding, social bonding and economy too. So far I have told the story of India "Inclusive" of its past and possibilities by learning from the past. Now I am willing to stay about the modernization of autarky into liberalization, or in simple "The Transition" Liberalization is the hallmark of flourishing and green economy.There is no boundation on it.It is a economics of free, open, "exclusive" while at the same time it is democratization which uphold the beauty of India as a liberal democracy.Generally it has been seen that in such classic example of democratic liberal economy and society.All the ban or regulation are relaxed and to get set a target to transit Inclusive things into exclusive economy.Let the parameter of India from J&K to kuchh of Gujarat to Goa, To Kerela to Odisa to North East to uttrakhand to himachal pradesh be recorded as the unmitigated and solidifying dessert, Himalaya, Forest, sea, ocean kutchh and so on. This natural boundation indicates that India is a country of diversity as well as per coalition by its destiny or future. I believe we have evolved and adapted such that we are eating the fruits of our unconditional support from echosystem.I am talking about this is because for a strong economy or a green economy.There is a need of exploring the treasure hidden by God in abundance in the nature, by the nature and of the nature.It has to be classified into three important pivot that you will read in next chapter.

CHAPTER TWO

IMPORTANT PIVOT

First is Inclusion:

As I earlier said how the economy of one of the oldest civilizational came into existance, & how economy become a tool of management into quality surfaced(for more detailing I suggest to read chapter1).

Second is mode (or medium) of trade and commerce.

Mode or medium is the solidified venture that allows or abstract or define the country's trade and commerce with the world economy, within or outside.It is that parameter which could be applied as the checkpoint or mode of transition, but it never allows any role of the outside world economy to take part in the economic fragilityand be regulated for instance from with Indian, industrial and investment policy, the medium serves about the business in terms of win-win circumstances.I believe the world was never so beautiful before in terms of business.

Now world over business is an art of settlement because now opportunities are there to settle the small countries got surveillance of big countries, such as Thailand, Maldives, Singapore, Egypt, Afghanistan, Pakistan and so on, and on surveillance there are big investors like USA, China, Russia, Uk, India, Japan etc.

All of them face problem in between but has a set of rules regulation to cope with any kind of situation.

What are the rules and regulations in India amid...?

Google says:"Foreign investment policies are for investing directly into production or business in a country by a company or a individual of another country.Investing may be buying a company another country or by expanding operations of the existing bn business in that country.The two main pegs of the investment is India is:

a)To sustain India's impressive economic growth foreign investment are necessary.
b)Protection of sectors which are of strategic interest such as defence and telecommunication".
There is not a single fuss about foreign investment in India.Actually foreign investment plays an anchor role for growth in India.Foreign investment policies(FIP) look through spectacles of

"Growth "and only "Growth"

We could only become developed and secured when growth engines are running in its full pace(This will be discussed in another chapter)
Another thing is defence equipment and telecommunication boom in India.these two sectors in India need to be highly confidential.So data about them not available.But my personal observation says without revealing the defence equipment manufactured in India by the medium of latest technology or telecommunication (defence and telecommunication are real brother.They are designed may be in Germany or France or USA, but when we made it in India it become ours.The prototype made possible the latest technology data warehouse are availed at defence equipment manufactured in India (I have turned on a flip-flop such that the two defence equipment and telecommunication togather achieve)...

Third is the external effect (or world view of Indian economy):-

An outside view of Indian economy is that now this to the investers call India, "Land of opportunity".I will not stop by saying only this but it is "Land of Possibilities".
If we lookIndia from external world or from outside view it is heaven for investment and investors,.As currently India eagerly looking at the world for business here, with a open heart to embrace the world and togather carry the sum of economy.

Let's talk about the reason, why is this development occur in India and who take over the guarantee and indulge to rule and regularise the economy.
First of all everyone knows that Dr.Manmohan Singh, P Chidambaram, Sam Pitroda and many distinguished leader hold the command of economy under the abled leadership of P V Narsimha Rao.To be more specific the

hero of liberalization was the then PM P.V Narsimha Rao and Dr. Manmohan Singh.They like the magician disappeared the garbage economy and come with fresh ideas and policies, their expertise was so accurate that after two years and so of Liberalization the Indian economy started regaining it's due and enhanced the boom of the economy, There is a lots of things to say about them that we will discuss in next few chapters).Now we will discuss why liberalization?The answer lied in thinking out of the box.Enough of trade barriers, tarrifs and red tape culture, license raj had made the economy of India stumbled and destabilized corrode the balance of trade unfortunately made impossible rebirth of economy.

In 1991 Liberalization was made the objectives to regain the economy by reshaping it and enabling some spoiled outdated rules and regulations or policies which could be called as garbage economy(or extracted garbage without any relevance of that time).Like grasping the fruit and still carrying the peel of and seeds unknowingly!

The most important thing of liberalization 1991 was it's reform oriented approach.Such reforms that ate only investigate the economic offences that are surfacing due to old methods and ways these are the key reforms of 1991:-

a)Exchange rate system,
b)Balance of payments problems,
c)Close to default resulting in bad foreign exchange,
d)We mortgaged 20 tones of gold in union bank of switzerland and 47 tones to UK as a part of bailout deal.These things we will discuss in next few chapters in length.

CHAPTER THREE

KIND OF REFORM NEEDED IN 1991

Here I will turn that page of history which tends about the real independent economy of India.In this chapter I will mark the details of "Exchange rate system".

Exchange Rate System

Financially an exchange rate is the term usually used to define the value of Currency, like value of one currency compared to the value of another currency.

Actually exchange rate are the laboratory of the financial system of a country specially in India.An exchange rate is the laboratory because should go through litmus test as a theory of give and take and turns the currency balancing equilibrium by Exchange.

In simple words exchange rate could be understood by simple example, like the exchange rate of Indian currency rupees (?) and US dollar($)In current exchange rate is, 1$ is equal to nearly 71.48 Rupees.This is how it could be understood to every comparison between world currency.

Why Exchange Rate?

Apart from exchange rate is the "Marker of market" driven by supply and demand exchange rate constantly change as floating exchange rate in the world getting reference from the International banks.In a short defination exchange rate is the "marker of market"driven by supply and demand in the/of the International market.

The question arises how it vary according to supply and demand.See everything in the world has intrinsic value decided according to royalty sometimes rareness and sometimes face value But the most important factor is how it make believe...

I found there are two ways to attend the exchange rate:-
1)By exchanging currency
2)By tarrif increment/decrement over goods imported/exported with a mutual alignment to get profit contributing to exchange rate.

In brief...
1)By Exchanging Currency:
Exchanging currency by attaining eauilibrium.Exchanging currency is the ultimate goal of the trade and commerce.It is actually the harbinger of the deal between two countries Stoke exchange we deal with the shares of private enterprises to get lowered or magnified.Here Price rise/fall according to the value of selling particular commodity w.r.t. it's name exchange rate could be actually related to Stoke market as if that point which gives power or membership to the hands of common people to participate in the selling/buying shares .This strengthen the currency of a country and make available the way forward the "economic journey"of the currency in accordance with world view.
2)By tarrif increment/decrement over goods imported and exported with a mutual alignment to get profit contributing to exchange rate:
There are market forces in a substantial economy.It is supported by exchange of currency in return for importing/exporting goods & comodity.It generally come under the trade and commerce.
Mainly the commodity or goods depend on import/export the imported goods come under the tax ensured with the custom duty from one international trade or intercontinental service.The import/export duty are called tarrifs.these tarrif are the reason why there established world trade by different countries under the light of IMF(International Monetary Fund).The main purpose of IMF is to monitoring the monetary fund, while checking the exchange with levysometimes, sometimes taxes.
The functioning of tarrif in the exchange rate is the reason for the rise and fall of the Stoke exchange and other related financial institution like RBI(Reserve Bank Of India) or its now integrated bank system recently introduced in India.

One more thing is that india holds a special place in the world economy at.current times.It is the fifth largest economy in the world.To this there are contribution of all financial institution as well as big MNC(Multi-National company)which takeover the business from India to world with the courage

to compete with the other strong Manufacturing firms)with localized as well as native or home advantage.The company who are investing are those from International company for instance Amazon, many aviation industrial firms, there are talks of bullet train and microsoft likewise on and on...
I think the main purpose should not be only exchanging currency, levying taxes on commodities or trading while matarial
There must be a courtesy that a liberal view of the "money can be understood"
By the trade deal and tarrif got a leaving objective so that there become a comfortable and supporting environment in world trade in exchange of not only currency alienation on the exchange of good also.This is my open view.

CHAPTER FOUR

BALANCE OF PAYMENT PROBLEM, (BOP PROBLEM)

The defination available in Internet says,
"The main cause of disequilibrium in the balance of payment arises from imbalance between export and import of goods and services, that is deficit or surplus in balance of trade...
If It is not matched by other items in the balance of payment disequilibrium will occur.

Balance of Payment problem in India:
Let me explain the Balance of payment problem in brief.So my observation is that disequilibrium in balance of payment in India is because of the imbalance on importing and exporting due to imbalance of "balance-of-trade".Actually balance of payment have a difference from Balance of trade but often students of economics carried away in the differentiating between balance of trade and balance of payment.
A balance of trade is disequilibrium between the import and export involved for goods.it is basically done as gOods merchant .While a balance of payment is directly related to the exchequer of the economy.In balance of payment their is a risk(disequilibrium)involved to the currency or the payment method whatever...
Here I will write about balance of payment.This is the subject to microeconomics . In balance of payment problem entities have vested interest to resolve the problem of disequilibrium in the wake of tarrif and exchange rate.Such disequilibrium was addressed in 1991 during the adverse condition for Indian economy. And the remedy was liberalization.
During that period of constant reforms requiring balance of payment (BoP)was such critical.As before liberalization in 1991, we were self default

economy in which we could not have the bussiness as usual in the world as in an open fashion.l liberalization was such frame that after only two years India become a growing economy remarkeably.Balance of payment is become a problem at the implementation level as it makes a implementation level as it makes a default statement in the running economy which created a problem of a self distortion due to limited frame work as problems, or risk or disequilibrium churn as the self frustrating loop, which deny the normal flow of the economy, which was open to all other developed and developing countrycountering inflows of investment at one time and outflows of investment at the other impulsive theory like a world force joined the investment in India, and India invested in the world trade as well within a time frame to Settle the economy in the do's and don'ts of the basic structure of our reform movement.

With all might Indian National Congress had chosen a PM Narsimha Rao, and his finance minister was Dr. Manmohan Singh.Rao along with Dr. Singh analysed and done the correct diagnosis, to let the economy on track.The serious BoP was haunting Indian economy with its tentacles or hands made up of core economical situations.Narsimha Rao in the one way took the government and politically census it, to be ready for change or liberalization with the consent of parliament and opposition.
On the other hand Dr. Manmohan Singh replied the economic emergency with firmness and regularity with short terms measures.Things fell in line of Narsimha Rao and Dr. Manmohan Singh.

Export rises and makes a surplus balance of trade and when import rises outshining export it causes deficit.In the June of 1991 it was the deficit which causes for such structural reform.

Necessary Structural Reforms In 1991:-

There are a stake of necessary Structural Reforms which was awaiting to be realized in Indian soil.There were Series of structural reforms from microsoft economics placed in the order.These reforms were International Oil and commodity prices reforms, goods and services, e exchange rate, all these pointed examples were the possibilities of structural reforms indication.In the back of it lies the reality variables which opened and shuted according to the above examples of survival of structural reforms.The back door of these variation lies the demand and supply tastes investment risk involved expectancy etc.Involving all these if one moves for change with changing the variables .It causes disequilibrium(risk or imbalance).

Microeconomic stability flourish when there is a coordination between it's factor and the impulsive force are designed to lower the risks through a work mechanism to adjust or simplify respectively; the international value on the basis of abundance & scarcity.

CHAPTER FIVE

THE COLLAPSED FOREIGN EXCHANGE

Close to default resulting in bad foreign exchange:

When the import and export two wheeler bicycle imbalanced (Disequilibrium) the economy suffers and close to default, when import is greater than export.

The problem further Rises to resulting in bad foreign exchange or we can say without export the currency got struck to a limitation and tends to bad foreign exchange further it can be called as the deficit Rises in the economy. This deficit Rises to the the the serious consequences foreign exchange means how much currency can buy another currency.At present 1 US Dollar is equal to the rupees 71 or more. Means to the exchange of $1 one can get get Rs 71 from foreign exchange institutions. In 1991 foreign exchange was in extremely bad shape. We were dealing with the debt crisis generated due to default resulting in bad foreign exchange. Foreign exchange also called as Forex is the symbol of its name which can be interpreted as exchange of currencies between the countries resulting in poor shape of one currency to the dear face value deteriorating condition of currency in compare to other is the reason for or bad and risked foreign exchange Or Forex.

According to moody's global credit policy:-
Forces affecting risk
Historically failure to make good on loans is a bigger problem four countries that borrow in a foreign currency. The reason is that when a country that borrows foreign currency faces a budgetary shortfall.It does not have the

option to print more money.

Many developing countries issue bonds in an alternate currency. Often the US dollar and wealth and the ability to borrow plays such a significant role in the the default risk. Once a country has defaulted once it become even harder to borrow in the future, so low income countries are particular at risk of default.

MY TAKE

Foreign currency like dollar deploys A beginning of the currency exchange. It gets the priority over any currency as it is in the strongest currency regarded as ...

If forex is the class then the monitor of class is US dollar and the the faculty are IMF and World Bank in this class Forex if there is no precision to take care of that each and every currency compared to the strong currency that is currency like US dollar, Pounds etc then there will be definitely a default in developing countries .It is the duty of the foreign currency to exchange notes each other this not only strengthen the foreign currency of the developing country but also the currency which is powerful and with no risk to be at default risk got more subtle and substantial in Forex.

The role of monitor is that to "define the default definitely in developing country". By definite default I mean that in a condition when there is a need of Fiscal discipline then the monitor need to take charge and maintain fixed foreign exchange in the forex.

Now we should come to the the IMF International Monetary Fund and World Bank who are the faculty to the Forex class the main role of faculty is the decision making and save the country from bailout and move on observation of their currency while in contrast with the Forex class. In 1991 the liberalisation of Indian economy was in the tune with the forex design that I have signalled and written in as class monitor and faculty (that is Forex ,currency, IMF and World Bank at that time all the economic indicators were showing down and there was a default risk causing debt and deficit. The fiscal discipline had in horror condition even Stock Exchange was doing badly the liberalisation with reserve Bank in 1991 was the positive movement at the right moment.

ROLE OF P. V. NARSIMHA RAO DURING LIBERALIZATION

PV Narasimha Rao was the 9th Prime Minister of the republic of India.He was a lawyer and politician. He was regarded as "the father of Indian economic reform".He was justified as Chanakya of modern India.Following the main reforms of liberalisation after 1991 onwards.

Abolishing in 1992 the controller of capital issues

The main reason to connect with the abolition controller of capital issue was to safeguard the share interest in generally and commonly. This was mainly to establish equilibrium, all this mean that there is a clocked controlled over the capital issues. The main motto of this was to get recognised and Limited the shares of a designated frms hair the step that and determined the value of each share keeping in mind the number of shares had in the limitation. Not just limitation but what should be the price of shares in the context also.

Introducing SEBI Act of 1992 and amendment of security laws

This give SEBI (security and exchange Board of India Act). The SEBI Act was introduced to verify every unknown and suspicious conditions activity which could effectively counter the stability of currency as well as stability of foreign exchange it also stop smuggling of gold and counterfeiting of currency. That way SEBI actually was the answer to the the hindrance in the national progress of India due to the effectiveness and all the rules having said that are looping impurity come into existence.Some of the laws are from 1947 and 1951, these laws are outdated and need to be filled or deleted from the memory. Pamulaparthi Venkata Narasimha Rao and Anchor role in formulating SEBI Act from the beginning of the idea to its implementation.The Chanakya of India politics saved India from being embarrassed in the world stage for lower GDP Gross Domestic Product and disastrous fiscal deficit.

Opening up in 1992 of India equity market to investment by foreign investors

See opening up in 1992 of India's city market was symbol of economic freedom to a extent. And because of this in India had broken rule of purely socialistic approach and gained a new height of capitalisticapproach.The approach was also said to be stock market or the capital market. In the equity market there is a balanced capital to be realized into currency formulation or formulated to stocks. I am afraid or risking to say that it may be called stalled market or stock market commodities are compared for sailing in the stock exchange. It is also placed in the regime of the foreign exchange their capital goods are turn up to foreign currencies and exchange of notes on the basis of investment policies to foreign exposure of growth in equity market to achieve unprecedented equilibrium.

Starting in 1994 all all the National Stock Exchange

After the 1991 reforms when GDP numbers and Expressable, National Stock Exchange was first to introduce computers.Here after a long battle in 1996 the NSE was formed by PV Narasimha Rao which was one of the biggest trading system that are fulfilling our wish till now, which was the main achievement of the ex-PM.

Reducing tariff

During the economic liberalisation tariff came under the Purchasable rate because it is reduced from 85% to 25%.For the first time rupee was made available in the world stage to be convertible or exchanged on trade account. Actually by reducing tariff for making Indian firms accountable to profit. PV Narasimha was the think tank behind the reduction of tariff or actually profit of import and export when average of tariff came under 30's to 25 from 85, thethen it was the signal for a open market for the foreign investments.

Encouraging foreign direct investment

Encouraging foreign direct investment is the core of liberalisation or one of the basic element of economy. FDI could hold hundred percent stock or equity in the priority sectors and the economy with the 40 to 51% of the joint share or investment claimed then, this was Mr Rao's most famous policy because after this India was become a global hub for investment of the foreign regime this breaks the rules of autarky and new investment of around 35 countries come to investment most of them where announced multinational companies this conflict of interest letter changed into competition in the market between local investment and foreign investment this all added to GDP or growth in the economy.

CHAPTER SEVEN

THE FAMOUS MAN FM OR THE FINANCE MINISTER

The famous man FM or the finance minister FM Dr Manmohan Singh during 1991 and onwards

If I say in Candid manner that FM Dr. Manmohan Singh during liberalisation was a Hero not because of his political will actually politics till today is a part time time job and and his man job was to work up on difficulties and narrowing parts of Economics stumbling Dr Manmohan Singh even after become prime minister.Doctor singh Singh failed theory of Mahatma Gandhi that to, "be the change that you want to see the world" but he defies this theory by doing not to be the change politically, his work first policy but changes the entire cabinet to a fruitful branches of trees(full of active politicians)

Dr Manmohan Singh role in liberalization is of the main character in India's growth story he played an anchor role along with P Chidambaram and PM Narsimha Rao and eventually back track the Indian economy. The threat was very serious India's fiscal deficit were closed to 8.5 % % of the GDP that means India was facing a severe financial and economic crisis 8.5 % of GDP means crisis bigger than our status quo India was only Dollar 1 billion economy in compare to US dollar 283 billion for importing commodity from foreign countries.Initially in 1991 India had resume of only two weeks of import Dr Manmohan Singh was told to hold the economy at the time or rate of depositing in gold likely to be his steps towards rejuvenating by being bold.

The balance of payment deficit too was used and unworthy of the title of balance because there was a certain imbalance causing there is severe loss likewise increasing exponentially with the increase in huge loss.The current account deficit was touching 3.5% of GDP which was too much to stop the movement and momentum of the India's regular economy. I used the term regular economy because after independence India was nowhere in the economic development , snatched by the British Empire On the name of economy that has only proud history of Golden period of Chandragupta Maurya and Ashoka.

On the name of Indian economy it was taking baby steps such as the the formation of Indian Republic constitution and planning commission and many things to introduced India to the term economy this is earned of Prime Minister and the Finance Minister forward.In 70's Indira Gandhi took about decision of Nationalising in banking system in India time passes and India economic get set to be matured for this situation. I use the term regular economy which was uninfluenced by the foreign investment and trade and Commerce and then it was only within its parameters and Manmohan Singh recognises this and open the norms to them to embrace the friendly liberalisation.

In the wake of liberalization the World Bank consider dollar 500 million bailout to India and inter national Monetary Fund supported thoroughly.But this was possible only because of the Trinity of the three means P Chidambaram, Dr Manmohan Singh and PV Narasimha Rao, in which the main role was played by Doctor Manmohan Singh as per international journals and reports .He presented the budget in 1991 and opened all gates of the economic river that come from foreign countries in the name of foreign direct investment

Challenges He Faced With Big Heart:-

One of the major challenges in budget 1991 by Dr. Singh was release Indian economy which was in the shell of gravity even if it has wings to fly higher and higher.

Secondly India has only 2 weeks for import from foreign countries must be the first priority to be handle in this scaring matter trade and Commerce was only regarded on paper the condition was sorting and getting worst , red carpet and licence Raj was boiling and the Indian market and economy was suffering within.

Thirdly was gold deposited to World Bank and IMF as a pledge, gold reserve was deposited because of the Twin deficit occurred due to the balance of payment deficit.

Key measures taken by Doctor Manmohan Singh to face the challenges

1. India mortgage gold as a security to go and and World Bank for the sanction of dollar 600 million loan.Actually it has to pay in terms of gold by 47 tons to bank of of UK and 20 turns to Bank of to Bank of Switzerland.

2. There was a catalytic transformation in the initial period of liberalisation to contain taxes and duties progressively. To attract foreign as well as native Industries to lower taxes and duties and tariffs to a control of procedure which can ease business sufficiently.

3. Thethen economy was opened for trade and Commerce, privatization and competition was encouraged in the Indian market.

All these things made Dr. Manmohan Singh the greatest reformer of all time in India's growth story.

CHAPTER EIGHT

P. CHIDAMBARAM THE ENERGY BEHIND THE LIBERALIZATION

Role of P Chidambaram in the trade & commerce sector formulating and formating for new design

A distinguished beginning(Introduction):

I must say P Chidambaram was the important architect of liberalization in 1991 because of his potential and competent nature.Apart from this it was mandatory that he was at his best in designing the reforms in early age.His high and capable business mindedness plus social understanding let him stood by soldier to soldier with Narsimha Rao, Dr. Manmohan Singh.

Today P Chidambaram is the most vibrant opposition leader now of India.He is the loyal son of the soil(India) from South India actually but also the proud member of congress party.These days he raises important issues in his compilation of weekly essays Across The Aisle which is a subject of matter to political, geo-political, economic, social, views for J and K and many such views where he is the front runner.We will get the details in next few chapters, but let's not change the vitality of 1991 reforms that changes the game for India which corelate with P Chidambaram hard work and distinguished leadership to contain the faith of Narsimha Rao and Dr. Manmohan Singh.Actually his working and performance effort is his natural instinct which is as simple crystal clear and at the level of high potential.

His way of dialogue & design:-

Like Modern India was evolving, Mr. Chidambaram also was evolving as a mature, decision maker, experienced, work-o- holic, kind, Hard labour and a beautiful mind and a fine person.His way of dialogue was about clinching the difference between Indian economy competitive to similar economies of the world like China, Brazil, Argentina, newly born economies like south africa, Egypt, Newzealand and so on...
I will not hesitate to write that he was the Indian inventor giving India idea irrespective of such a diverse country carrying as whole total to be upgradef to simplify economy w.r.t developed economies.His thinking was India must develop from its core issues to a more plural, rationalized, modern, nationalized and united like developed countries.His vision was exact like he want India being in future, I believe he is 70% satisfied and happy by the developing India and it's care takers i e government accordingly.

He had a clear design for trade and commerce for India as a commerce minister during liberalization.He identify the need to expansion of like minded economies, later because of his effort submission like G-20, BRICS etc were formulated.Mr. Chidambaram was the most familiar face of India after the ministery of foreign affairs.
His trade policy was to keep motivating Investors from and outside India and to bridge the gap between--to locate India's position regarding foreign Investment and investers within to cultivate a business atmosphere which could attract the opposite ends complementing the investor and the investment venture destination.These were the resources available for it which were classified in three categories as follows:-

a)Applying Human resource:Mr. Chidambaram had invented a unique way to amplify the human resources with mechanical operationalized by the latest technology of that time.Human resource were advanced to operate technicalities of the time with mechanical punch.Today when India is in deep crisis of joblessness , and low GDP, we don't need to shut down we need to find opportunity in it by invigorating more opportunities and expansion fro it's core like Jupiter's atmosphere differentiated with dust, clouds , outer ring with 12 moon.To attract competitive investment don't be like Earth, which is followed by all, but be attractive, Volatile, syrupy atmosphere and the biggest planet in solar system.I want India to follow the order or justify Jupiter model.

b)Focus on business returning the politics and local factors to re-energize the principle investment:
See there was a ultimate factor 'Risk' involved within the system running at that time.No country believe easily on India because of old customs, and way of trade &commerce.There was red tapism, voice of licence raj, risk of social security, corruption in system, and so on...
P Chidambaram not only understood these core issues but could be said he was one of the main reformer to India's business strategy and ideal investment.

c)Market nerves(graphs):
P Chidambaram had a unique quality of reading the nerves of the market.He was the one who introduced market stability in terms of development in correspondence with foreign market stability.He set the target to transform India's market liquidity to remain... and don't get freezed in foreign environment.Market competency was at its peak at that time when liberalization a process not the click of a button.Mr. Chidambaram had clinched the market strategy to be filled with hope, and fearless spending or investment in trade which further raised above the critical point in the experimental basis to a new standard of which changed the principle investment and respect of the market changing the odds and myths to start a market advancement culture, which is also the requirement of vastly developing India as a totality not the partial behaviour in favour to certain market game changers.

CHAPTER NINE

SAILING EFFECTIVELY WITH THE WIND

The economy of a developing country cannot be just defined in the measure of its growth rate but it does not interpret that growth can be subsidized or minimized or justified even if the growth remain accelerating or even de accelerating, unless or until it is movable or mobile.

It has the capacity to get rebuild everytime it falls or everytime it raises abruptly.

A balanced growth rate in a country like India, especially after Mr. Modi took over is not a real possibility.It is a hard truth.This is because growth is apparent, it has been builded throughout.Any economic parameter fluctuation can actually hurt the economic growth.Actuall all I want to see is that it is a blessing in disguise which has created the space for probable outcomes which is pre-fragile, and can attain a positive number may be 10% in one quarter and 6.5% in another quarter.Eventually which could be resolved to 8.5% GDP which is not bad at all.This is the dynamics of economy in India or new India, but attaintively government is slow, very slow indeed in taking bold measures which led to less performing economy especially fluctuation towards the good no's that is 9 to 10 % GDP in any quarter.

Need of the hour is to let the economy move or walk by itself, may be initially it require crutches but ultimately I hope it will walk by own as the as the terms and condition are favourable to higher as well as lower points of the fluctuation.

At the end I will say economy must be in the auto-pilot mode and checked when it is taken down and celebrated when elevated both at the mean time, when it is subjected to growth residing inside or modus operandi in the auto pilot mode.

This could be the new normal to attain a considerable growth worthwhile the only thing govt. has to do is to Sail Effectively With The Wind.

CHAPTER TEN

SAILING EFFECTIVELY WITH THE WIND-2

Don't juggle or shuffle:-

The most alarming situation is here; the economic slowdown.What should a govt. Could do.As a opposition voice I will say don't suffle or juggle the economy, otherwise the economy become out of order, and sustainable growth which will definitely make the economy rise would be deprived of the basic growth which can be attainable even if there is no ministry for finance: that is in default case.I am not saying completely depend on order of the economy but to be partial in common steps or juggle it for business purpose is the wrong direction or defensive economy.

How to achieve order in a juggling or shuffling economy:-

When it turns to find out the cause of slowdown in growth I will blame the govt's for not giving honour and stabilize the downfall of economy w.r.t. budget order.

To revive economy their should be juggling and do business as usual but we should not loose the default line and loose also what we could have...

I mean stability at the base but business in the face!Govt. Need to think how it could balance and attain order when facing juggle and suffle in the economy.Actuall both are the part of economy but need to understand how we can be constructive or economy building or additive.

Separate the necessary from the unnecessary:-

One of the major setback causing the downfall of economy is adulteration in the usual business of the manufacturing and set infrastructure development.Manufacturing is at record low need to be addresses immediately and garner it from the raw business or market.This sense that the liquidity required in manufacturing and infrastructure development and raw left to revitalise and gain business confidence.

Auto sector require a positive market which could be attended as loose parts buyers, If they are not buying new than approximately they need the new parts to revive their old one's.So they may not assemble new one but manufacture parts prone to be used in older vehicles.Therefore encourage to build body parts in the win win situation.

Job is in great crisis.A jobless growth is nothing but the work laden economy.Job loss not only bad for the jobless youth in the one hand but attack the market with all its might lowering GDP in the other hand.Therefore creating exponentially downward loop trend.

I hope the FM will find a eagerly needed questions raised by time through me.I also hope when I write another blog next week India will acquire and arrange for better than current situation.So stop making excuse and execute effectively.

CHAPTER ELEVEN

IF THEY MAKE ME FM FOR A DAY

The first thing I will do if they make me FM for a day is that I will break the monotonous approach of the government.Continuity is a important thing but at some point it breaks if it is not flexible.We must recognize that critical point while address and fix it with suitable steps.Indian economy under BJP is fragile.The reason behind the decline of economy after demonetization is it has directly exposed the economy to crude and rude market.Its implications are, reform become stagnant resulting in the direct affect on the SME sector and consequently people looses jobs all over India.There are no job or it is not wrong that India is in a decline of job growth or its production.

The second thing I would do is change the the atmosphere of investment in India.For growth it is a bookmark that we need investment from wherever and however it come from.But the current situation is that government has made a firewall to protect the economy which in turn foolishly acts as a scaring zone for the investors.Now let us talk about govt. efforts.Make in India was a jumla(gimmick), a half hearted approach which lands India nowhere in the growth story, as a FM I would have make investments the bread and butter for the indian economy.Even if they say they are ready to MoU a import based investment but not actually as import but like it does not affect Indian share and Indian market even though they have production line in their own country.Some technicalities can be improved in this manner such as the environment that we are unable to inculcate in our country for the investments.In easy words we could invest in foreign lands to get the foreign investment for the sake of our economy.

The third thing I would do is open the gates of reforms.India seriously need reforms in all sectors.BJP govt. has failed in reforming India even after getting such mandate.We seriously need to check economic reforms.Current account deficit has increased to a level that is seriously need a tap to lower it down by making a policy change like making imports and exports more volatile that it could automatically checked in the process.The another thing that can be done to lower current account deficit is to relying on investment in smaller economies after importing from big economies.In current policies of the govt. This is normal that it could not anchor the fiscal deficit.If they make me FM I would stop small reckless spending and push forwards the big investments.

Reforms also need in our bureaucracy so that their could be a transparent governance.In BJP government it is a fact that middle hierarchy or bureaucrat is the most corrupt order after independence, if I am a FM for a day I would have a online conference with all the bureaucrats of India, and question them about their integrity or about their lower order.I would have reviewed smart city project and many other reforms that were suspended or stalled in the beginning phase.

People are watching all the failures of govt. patiently and BJP is thinking they are making fool out of them.So be prepared for the people's court which is supreme than all other.

Although I have said if they make me FM for a day.But my purpose is completely to realize this govt. of reality and not to taste the FM chair and also to let them know that common man can hold a view which is open and factual like a hindi movie said "Don't underestimate the power of a common man".

CHAPTER TWELVE

OUR ECONOMY AND IT'S POTENTIAL

The economic potential of our country is diverse but adjoined. India have one of the biggest market in the world of business.This diverse and adjoined economic potential allows it to be concentrate as the circumference throughout its big market.The current economic distribution is such that we have to

collectively respond with the change in its fluid structure, which give it a special place and resistance in the changing world economy.I must say, our economy have a detailed growth story, providing it to maintain at the top growth rate in spite, we are still a developing nation.But it is not the last level

we are still in a position to evaluate our economic growth rate to 9% to 10% then only we will be able to consolidate with the developed economies of the world.Let us look at some briefing of infrastructure development, manufacturing and fiscal deficit and how RBI and banking sector relates on the go..

Our infrastructure development is the concrete step towards the reach of well suited environment for the growth, versus the stalled or stranded projects converging it to the unstable focal point. Infrastructure relocates the power handling of projects to invigorate the development process to undermine with the

basic strategy to the entropy of Indian market.The randomization of development is the inertia or theme to inculcate the infrastructure development.When we talk about manufacturing, we determine to our policies that cast to give a shape to our nation building process.India has become a manufacturing

hub as it has the capacity to have a essential availability, a supporting environment and a good marketplace.I believe manufacturing should seems to have a proper drilling to capture the investments to a responsible level, and seek a resultant solution to be present at all stages to resolve the problems.

Our fiscal deficit denotes our need of quick recovery of our economy, Although we have improved a lot in this section but there is a need to be a fair enough improvisation. Our fiscal policies are volatile in nature because it recommends the substantive up-gradation but i think it should be more factual in

its appetite, so that the adequate space should be granted.RBI's governing policies are like hallucinating pills to the banking sectors that states sufficient life to them but requires greater energy to give its that special impulse to excel.RBI current policies meets the government policies in the fashion of needs and emergency which should be more involving, may it could be opposing each other.I feel our economy is in the middle of big change in next few years.Government has able to attract foreign investment and magnetizing its economic field by using some of the plans like Make in India, Start up India etc.let's have a look at these two steps of this government.

Make in India is the step towards need of process based development of India.Make in India is an exposure of Indian big market field to the world to initialize manufacturing in a stable and good environment.while some believe, Make in India is the total fencing of the Indian market with respect to the foreign market.we can also call it as a net evaluation of capable work field of our country.One another step towards encouraging Indian business is to make new entrepreneurship and it is called as start up India.Start up India provides the platform for new entrepreneurs. It is an idea to take an avatar to turn the business with an interesting support while contributing to the Indian economy and its vast potential.

CHAPTER THIRTEEN

INDIA AND OUTSIDE

Foreign policy of a country depends on diplomatic ends one is the engine of transparency between the nations and the reciprocal, the secrecy persist in the fashion.Foreign policy directs the diplomatic channels of the national interest.The world is integrated by the threads of foreign policies of different nations.Foreign policy gives the required thrust to the socio-economic and cultural environment of the world. At a glance the world politics seems to be adjusting in nature but the balance is far more critical in impacts and deeds due to co-ordination dimension of relationship emerging from different nations for the common interest.Then the question arises what is the international significance of the sweet and bitter relationships between as Asia and American continents and the value of Europe, Africa and Australia in the midst(this we will discuss later). while in, where does India stands in its foreign relationships.

India's Foreign Policy

India's foreign policy is mild and simple since independence and the-then Prime Minister pt. Jawahar Lal Nehru was the torch bearer of it. We intended and were the founder of non-align countries during the time of cold war.Now the world politics has changed by the time or it is better to say that the world

politics has become harder in the context.India has also changed its concern over the time, we have illustrated democracy across the world and help developing it in many other nations.Indian subcontinent has geo-political aspects of regional effects as it is surrounded with its neighbors from all the sides.In world politics India has less interventions but it has a key role in the decisiveness of social and political justice in the world affairs.All the way we have a friendly relation with all the nations with no considerable strife we are heading and leading a peaceful nation.My opinion regarding India foreign policy with most of the country is based on the quite leading and forward in nature.India can play a major role in deriving the world crisis in a substantial manner such as by supporting the local leaders and general people in the war prone and vulnerable places.What is going in middle east and Syria is well known to everybody but India can cast its view and convey the thinking of the common people in the international front.Anyway I want to discuss India's relationship mainly with two countries here i.e, Pakistan and China, where India remain concerned...

India and China

India has a detailed Foreign policy with china.Although good relation with china is important for India but we deal with mixed thoughts too.What I feel about china is that they have adopted a one way talk to the outer world. Their foreign policy revolves around the unjustified or one way objective to the rest
of the world.In fact they have full right to do so but the concern is when they don't feel and aspect the same from other countries.Also China have a interesting directive of being called as a superpower; fascinated from United states.India and china is mutually dependent with social and economic ties with each other, we are serving china as the biggest market for the Chinese firms.I believe India should do a total makeover with China by making a separate single Chinese business corridor to strengthen its economic ties for mutual benefit.We have border issues too with china which I think is due to the wealthy democracy in India and China self defined democracy.Certainly China's friendship to India is that they are also not war supporters like India.

India and Pakistan

World knows what is the idea of India's relationship with Pakistan.We are a strife prone neighbors from the day of separation.We have witnessed many wars and war like intrusions many times.India and Pakistan both suffer in these fight over the piece of land called Jammu and kashmir.I believe Jammu and Kashmir
is in India's forehead that no one could apart.India has tried to make a good relation with Pakistan many times but failed because of Pakistan's

phenomenon of replying in their own tuned definition of achieving points to make Kashmir an international agenda.In this course they have been isolated many times due to self destructing image in the world stage.Our govt hold talks in between but short ripples disappears soon when big waves arises.India and Pakistan have not so considerable trade commitment still we found ways to be comfortable in this zone of Asia.

CHAPTER FOURTEEN

OUR COUNTRY INDIA

The penetration of Indian democracy into its future and depth of Indian democracy in the past, both circumstances are fusible and required to form a civilized nation.The nationalist thoughts are the mercury droplets that decides the degree of nation building and its reforms. Then, why Indian democracy is
mix and still unique? The answer is within its vastness of culture, thoughts, diverse land, different religion and different lifestyle but one single nationality and this is Indian nationality.India is a store house of ductile and preserved thoughts due to its glorious past, descent present and i am sure of its tremendous future.Our civilization is one of the oldest and valuable in the world map which is progressing with its independent core of permeation of thoughts and deeds.Our Civilization values are the course of our spiritual development and rationalized wisdom as a world leader.Our democracy dwells in the universal brotherhood and traditions.It assembles the freedom of thinking,living and light and breaks the barriers of darkness and violation.

Backbone of Indian democracy

When we think about the backbone of Indian democracy the only subject comes in our mind is Indian politics.Politics is the multiplicity of simplicity.Politics is the longevity of life cycle of a democracy.Indian politics have both these quality of simplicity and longevity without any dubious doubts of
unworthiness. The entropy of our political system is instinctive in its core nature as we have diversity in counters of development.Our political structure is such that it automatically verify any intrusions coming to exploit out political unit culture. A political system should be a support of

its tradition,
culture and human values.It must engulfs all kinds of discrimination which probably raising in the distinct societies.It is also the image of our generational intentions to make India free from all insecurities and allow it to thrive at its best.But, then we have shortcomings too which needs to be sort out in a fascination of giving it a limitation.We have two major political parties in our country, Indian Natinal Congress(UPA) and Bhartiya Janata Party(NDA).I think congress is a political party of defined exposure, its problem is at certain level it is unable to control the overexposure of its party.

While the BJP is a party of deep roots and well intrinsic but the problem arises when it is unable to balance it to the present context. After all in politics one have to be sure and confident in ups and down.

Revolving constitution

If politics is the backbone then, constitution is the life line of Indian democracy.Constitution revolves around the democratic system and make sure the normalization of the procedural activities.Constitution is a laying foundation of our political and constitutional structure, which totally acknowledge
the federal definitions up to its requirement.Our constitution is made up of well suited derivations and solidarity.The constitution makers had kept in mind the subtle and sublime configurations of distinct priorities.The general thing for a well defined constitution is the well addressed directives of the
enduring indexes that should be in the order of challenging behaviors going all the way.

The analogy of Flexible India

There is no doubt that India is a flexible nation breaking all its stubborn visuals.The analogy relies on the surreal extensions of its development after independence.India developed in all its dimensions, We are the largest democracy progressing at the highest growth rate at present.The analogy also revives
and roving the vastness of its progressive integration.The analogy of flexible India reflects the body line of the Indian developmental insights.In total,

India is a place of royal realities onto dim dreams.

CHAPTER FIFTEEN

DIFFUSING TERRORISM(few stories)

Terrorism is the term given to unwanted extremist and violence activity of the people claiming the belonging of certain religion.I call it belonging of religion, because it will be wrong to declare them as the wisdom or habitats of certain religion. In current scenario or in general if we look at it, one perspective is that some rebel group from the Islam is practicing terrorism. And it is not totally wrong to say this.

WHEN IT HAD ALL STARTED?

Terrorism at first started against to counter wars.It can also be called as the revenge to wars.The origin of terrorism is to gain the political revenge in parts of Europe. Then, many religious group started extreme violence in the shorter format as the substitute to extreme religious thoughts.Now,
some Islamist group are at the first place to take it as the magical weapon to fight against mightier countries.They found it easier and valuable to diversify their expansion of thoughts and religious views.Their point of view is clear, prove their point of view by terrorism through killing innocent people.There are also some other religion based terrorist group but not as active as in the people belonging to Islam.

The plane hijack and collision with world trade center and other buildings in US on 9/11/2001.
On September, 2001, a major terrorism activity had happened.Terrorists hijacked the Us plane and hit the world trade center and other buildings.Terrorist organization 'Al Qaeda' had taken the responsibility of the attack, who's leader was Osama-ben-laden.9/11 attack was the open

declared war with US.

It was the terrorist activity to suppress the power and supremacy of the super power, United States of America.Then obviously, the Us strikes back in search of Osama-ben-laden and its group in Afghanistan.Or we can say it was the war with Afghanistan to kill Osama.It had proved to be the one of the demolishing war

and final, but worth nothing because there real culprit was hidden somewhere in Pakistan, that they found it later and succeeded to punish him.Also his killing has diffused the Al Qaeda to some extent.9/11 attack was disturbing because it had killed thousands in USA then its aftermath had killed thousands

in Afghanistan.The terrorist activity and the war was for nothing but the approval of framing a fancy war from one side to a declared war to a nation by a powerful nation to demolish a terrorist group and subsequently maintain its position in the world.In whole it was the disclosure of new kind of war strategy after world war two.

The 26/11/2008 Mumbai terror attack.

Mumbai terror attack was carried out by the terrorist group from Pakistan named Lashkar-e-taiba on 26,September, 2008.It was a multiple terror attack at multiple places in Mumbai.The aim of the attack was to spread terror for their demand of liberated Kashmir.108 people were killed in this attack and

several injured. Indian forces also hit back and all the terrorist were killed and Ajmal Kasab was arrested, he finally revealed all the information about the attack and the role of Pakistan in the attack.Mumbai terror attack was the clear message that the Pakistan is totally indulge in terrorist activity and maintaining a proxy war against India.The main motivation of Mumbai terror attack was clearly came from the remainder of delusional terror outfit to dismantle the normal life in India on the name of Jihad.

The Kashmir issue...

Kashmir has been the apple of discord between India and Pakistan.Pakistan wants to capture the Kashmir more than anything else. But loyalty of Kashmir as an integral part of India is prominent.Due to this Pakistan has launched a terror program against India and mainly Jammu and Kashmir.There had been war

days between both the countries but the solution remains...

Very often there are terrorist encounter happen in Kashmir then the result is only an unstable Kashmir.The solution to the problem lies within the people of Kashmir where the democratic system is well suited and presently run by the elected government.Kashmir is not a divided issue rather it is considered as

a united issue for India.And the analyzing point of this problem is the conversion of the preserved talks into deeds where all things needs to be kept with agreement, then only the answers will be found.

CHAPTER SIXTEEN

THE REAL TRIUMPH

The real triumph of a economy can be defined in three stages, the one way reform, the expansion transition, the middle path of deal.

The one way reform

The one way reform suggests the straight economic paradise having a similar kind or one progressive economy of single minded zeal of the reformers.One way reform does not signify that it is not wide-spread, it has been equally evolving and developing in the growth in a descent manner.The growth is not only

meaningful but also substantial.As it is one way reform it advocates there are no U-turns which could create confusion in the long run.The vitality of economic growth is phenomenal due to the direct transaction of human force and developmental efforts of the differentiated trade keeping the negative factors

like inflation down under the controls of reformers.The inflation is such a depressing parameter that it engulf the stand of the economy.A well suited trade and commerce stumble under the effect of inflation.In India the most disturbing thing in the food inflation which raises the price of all food commodity to a painful level for the people.But the solution lies within itself, the requirement is to reach to the small business holders and to fulfill their priorities.The question arises; what is the priority?The priority is the rationalization of commodity.This could be the ground level direction to curb food inflation.The other important parameters in one way reform are the banking and finance which have derived from the RBI's policy making.RBI should have the policy to comfort the bank and finance by shunting the congestion of international market.

The expansion transition

Now, the expansion transition, is the risk taking phase of the economy.Risk taking phase in the sense that the economy is vulnerable in the growth and sluggishness endangered the rate of growth.The positive thing in the expansion transition is the reach and inclusion of the the last person, it can also be called as the dark phase as there is not direct involvement of any particular.The transition is bulky, diverse but significant in its approach to the India's growth story.Due to the low growth the matrix of the economy remains unstable and could not find the suitable answer to the parameters like inflation, fiscal deficit, banking and finance sector and others.In the course, the clearance of all delusional objectives to certain figure is must.

The middle path of deal

In the case of middle path of deal, the economy is in the hand of conciseness and consciousness. This can also be called as the smart economy.The economic growth in this category is socially and politically true.I call it true because there is no economic breakdown here.While in the case of one way reform and

the expansion transition there are major breakdown at the regular intervals.The middle path of deal, remain the functional agent in the growth. It divides the vulnerability of the economic growth and headed to a new progressive altitude.The progressive altitude is the degree of extension of the parameters of

the economic environment.The inflation in this case is also subtle. The inflation air do not disturb much the normal growth.Food inflation is at the little upper level but under the control.Banking and finance is totally recovering in the course of RBI's policies, which are providing space to them.Whatever be

the situation Indian economy has a supreme law, that it will be flexible in all time.